NO-QUESTION GUARANTEE

Braige Books, the publisher of
The Unchained Worker, *is confident that you will find this*
book to be worth far more than your purchase price. If for
any reason you do not agree, we will refund your full
purchase price, no questions asked.

We make this unusual offer because
we firmly believe The Unchained Worker *author*
Jeffrey Petkevicius when he writes, "When we
stop looking for someone to blame and
focus on ourselves, a wonderful surge of
positive energy and activity invigorates the soul.
Give Ownership a try and you'll
never look back."

Look at what people just like you are saying about
The Unchained Worker, Principals Of Ownership In The Workplace

"I've always believed in the individual's desire to succeed. Creating the right environment is the key. Ownership will work in any organization. GREAT STUFF!"
– Dennis Erickson, *Head Coach, Seattle Seahawks*

"Concise and to the point. A must for every working person. Easy reading. Anybody who works can relate to Ownership."
– Frank Albi, *Operations Manager*

"Ownership works! I've been using it for 25 years and never expressed it in terms as usable and dynamic as J.P."
– Kip Lachner, *President, Flextron Systems Corporation*

"Ownership offers readers a practical means of improving their performance and, in so doing, expands their career opportunities, accomplishments and rewards."
– Marshall J. Burak, Ph.D., *Dean, College of Business San Jose State University*

"The story of my life, just do it. Touches everyone who works."
– Chris Beason, *Test Engineer*

"Refreshing! Makes you feel good and have hope for the future. ALL RIGHT!!"
– Shirley Vesser, *Production Line Supervisor*

"The best motivational reading for an employee ever! Interesting and educational both for my job and family. If I'm a doer of Ownership, I'll never have to worry about my job, no matter how much down-sizing takes place."
– Neal Davis, *Engineering Manager*

"Send it to my boss, PLEASE!"
*– **Peggy Weathermon,** Production Line Assembler*

"What is right is not always popular, and what is popular is not always right. To do a good job at work, you need to remember that the more knowledge you gain, the more valuable you become. Ownership is the key."
*– **Ramadan Eshtewi,** Systems Engineer*

"Inspirational! Fantastic! What a wonderful book. It made me think about things I've never considered. Thanks."
*– **Staci Clevenger,** Assembly Line Worker*

"Ownership holds a great deal of truth."
*– **Steve Cianci,** Marketing Manager*

Frank,
Best wishes
always. It was
Great meeting you!

The
Unchained
WORKER

JEFFREY C. PETKEVICIUS

The Unchained WORKER

PRINCIPLES OF OWNERSHIP IN THE WORKPLACE

BRAIGE BOOKS

The Unchained Worker
Principles of Ownership in the Workplace

A Braige Book
Published by Braige Books, a division of Cybernetix Inc.

Published in the United States of America by:
Braige Books, a division of Cybernetix Inc.
14817 N. Jennifer Rd.
Mead, WA 99021
(800) 517-4268
email: OWNERSHIP@aol.com

Library of Congress Catalog Card Number 94-80013
ISBN: 0-9645204-3-5
First Edition

Author: Jeffrey C. Petkevicius
Editor: Dwain Smart
Graphics: Sean Maloney
and Marvin Reguindin
Cover Design: Sean Maloney

*This book
is dedicated to
my daughters,
Brooke and Paige.
They, and
the world's children,
are the future.*

TABLE OF CONTENTS

If

you were

the company owner,

how would you

change

your job?

CHAPTER 1

TAKE

CONTROL

OF

YOUR FUTURE

WITH

OWNERSHIP

What is Ownership?

What will Ownership do for me?

Why is it crucial for me to embrace Ownership?

One definition of insanity is doing the same things over and over again and expecting different results. Today's workplaces are just that – insane. Companies are doing the same things over and over, expecting different results, and failing. They're faced with global competition, buyouts, emerging markets, the explosion of technology, and more. The business climate has never been more volatile. Within the corporate and industrial walls, jobs are no longer fulfilling. Workers are disgruntled. There's no independence, no initiative, and it's all compounded by the fear of reductions, down-sizing or right-sizing. Layoffs are becoming a way of life. No job or business is secure.

Ownership can change all that.

WHAT IS OWNERSHIP?

What is Ownership? It's a new perspective for all of us to use when dealing with our jobs. Ownership is a mind-set, an attitude that forces you to look no further than yourself to secure your future in the workplace. It's the catalyst for superior individual performance within companies. It provides a common vocabulary for workers to excel as individuals. Ownership motivates people to develop their talents and bolster individual performance. It puts success in their hands.

For companies, Ownership helps structure and develop jobs that harvest individual talents. Companies that foster the Ownership philosophy will succeed in the fastest paced, most dynamic global business environment ever. Ownership makes people *want to* maximize their training and talents. From top to bottom, it unleashes the powerful, latent potential of every worker.

Ownership. It isn't a difficult concept. "I own it. I own it." Just say the words to yourself. What we're talking about is that gut feeling you have when you own *it*. Whatever *it* is, *it* is a part of you, your life. You want to be proud of *it*. You want *it* to be a positive reflection of who you are. Your house, your car, your job, whatever *it* is, is a statement about you. It's not really who you are, but it's a reflection of what you care about, what's important to you, and what you've worked for.

History is full of examples that prove people care more about what they own. Owning something satisfies the spirit. It makes you feel in control, despite the fact that it doesn't give you complete control. For instance, home Ownership is very satisfying to most but it doesn't carry exclusive or unconditional rights. Police, firemen and other officials may, under certain conditions, enter your home. You can't destroy your home or add to it without permission (permits) from local governments. But you still get a great sense of satisfaction from your home because you *own* it.

In the work arena, Ownership uses that same feeling of satisfaction to create a new relationship between employers and employees, where dedication and commitment to the  company's success is not isolated at the top of the organization. Everybody is committed to making their team succeed. It becomes a slight modification of what President John F. Kennedy once said to all Americans: "Ask not what your company can do for you (or what you can do for your company), but what your company and you can do for each other."

WHY IS IT CRUCIAL FOR ME TO EMBRACE OWNERSHIP?

How does Ownership benefit the individual and not just the company? To start, it's an employers' market. Employers have more people to choose from when filling jobs. As a result, companies are more selective about whom they hire. Higher levels of education and experience are becoming a part of every job opening. What this means to you and me is that we have to become indispensable employees. We have to be such valuable assets that, in essence, we become truly irreplaceable. If you need proof, consider the numbers:

- Since 1980 the workforce has expanded from 106.9 million workers to 125.3 million in 1991.
- The estimates for the year 2000 are 142.9 million available workers, up another 14 percent.[1]
- Worse yet, business failures increased from 50,361 in 1990 to 60,432 in 1991, up 20 percent in just one year.[2]

If you finally get through the difficult selection process for a job, you better do everything possible to help your company succeed.

Otherwise you'll wind up back in the pool of highly competitive job seekers. Now, more than ever, what benefits the company, benefits the individual.

The same holds true for businesses. The old top-down, paternalistic, family corporate days are over. A new model is taking hold that relies on inter-dependencies between companies and the people that do the work. Ownership is a requirement to survive the transition into the workplace of the twenty-first century.

If it's to be, it's up to me will be the credo for the twenty-first century. Our ability to survive will be in *our* hands, not the Union, not the mother company, but in our own hands. The only job security will be the value our personal skills bring to companies in need of them. Even if we're working inside a larger company, our jobs will be viewed as integrated independent business operations, from the janitor all the way up to the Chairman of the Board. More and more, we're going to be evaluated on the profit and loss potential of the services we provide. If there's a more efficient, economical way to do our job, the change will be swift and heartless, as many of us have already experienced.

The key, then, is to view ourselves as though we were all independent businesses. Would we thrive, survive or fail in the market? How can we improve the way our jobs are done to be more profitable? By doing so, we'll acquire skills as individuals that will allow us to grow our expertise and provide options about our future that *we* control (figure 1).

Ownership is a journey, not a destination. Here is a road map that will be your guide.

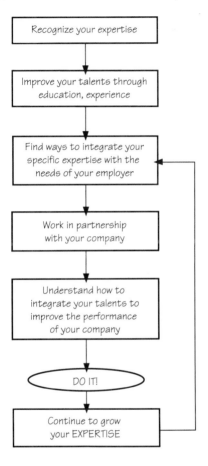

(figure 1)

Whether you actually branch out and start your own company is irrelevant. The point is that your perceptions of what you do, and why you do it, need to change. You need to step up and become an owner in your mind. Don't wait for big brother to figure it out for you, he doesn't exist anymore. It's up to you.

This sounds scary, and it is. But it's better to be scared now, take action and make the necessary changes, than to be left out in the cold without options in the future. Hopefully, you're working for a company that sees the benefits of Ownership and uses them. Even if you don't, by applying the concepts, you'll blossom into a star performer and an **Expert** in your job. You'll also be happier as an individual.

In Summary:

It's time for everyone, companies included, to step up to the table. Somewhere, somehow, we've evolved into a society that allows old ways of doing business to define who we are, which perpetuates zero personal accountability. In our work lives, personal lives and public lives, there's *somebody*, or *something*, to blame for everything that goes wrong. When something negative happens, we won't rest until that "somebody" is put to justice. It surely isn't our fault. Every time we point the finger, however, there are three fingers pointing right back at us.

Now is time to recognize that all of us are accountable for our happiness, successes, failures and misfortune. We own our lives. To start the process, we need to become owners of our expertise. We need to build and train in order to contribute to a partnership with companies. We need to look at our jobs as something we control, over which we have the authority to make decisions. ***Ownership inspires and motivates us to take action to protect and improve what's ours. We own our talents, experience and capabilities. When we put them in partnership with a company, the future is ours to make.*** It's time to live in an Ownership environment.

Give Ownership a try and you'll never look back.

WHAT WILL OWNERSHIP DO FOR ME?

As you learn and apply the concepts of Ownership, here's what you can expect to happen:

- Believe it or not, you'll look forward to Monday mornings. You will actually *want to* go to work. Your job will become enjoyable, rewarding and fulfilling.

- You'll build the foundation for your future. The type of job you have, the money you make and who you work for are *your* choice, not someone else's.

- Your authority will match your responsibility. The catch-22 of being responsible but not having the authority to decide will be eliminated. What you're responsible for, you'll have the authority to decide.

- Overlapping responsibilities will be eliminated. Jobs will be structured by what you own, and the person "in charge" of getting the work done is clear and specific.

- Problems don't go away; they will just be resolved faster by the people in the best position to make the decision and implement the solution.

- You, your co-workers and managers will establish a true TEAM that supports each other, in an effort to achieve greater goals than you could by yourself. There will be a high level of respect for everyone in your company.

- Your new environment will be charged with excitement and optimism. If you've ever been around famous athletes, actors or professionals of any kind, you can feel the confidence they have in their area of expertise. Ownership develops experts at every level, in every position in the company.

- Trust will develop between the boss and workers. Communication will represent a completion of work rather than a request for approval.

- People will solicit input from one another, including the boss. They will encourage input and criticism to increase their sphere of knowledge. As their knowledge base expands, so will their ability to generate effective solutions to problems. Input will be valued as a decision-making tool and heavily solicited.

- People will be motivated to offer input without worrying about their performance or personal career goals. The threat of political backfiring will be eliminated.

- The exchange of honest, unfiltered opinions will be prevalent. It will be understood that none, some, or all input may be used in making decisions. It will also be understood that the person vested with the decision-making responsibility is the best person to make the call.

- The decision-making process will become more efficient. The *right* people will be making the *right* decisions at the *right* time.

- People will have a reason to stay with the company. They will know that their individual talents and skills will be recognized and applied to the goals of the group and rewarded.

- Superstars will come out of the woodwork. People at all levels in the company will recognize what they have to contribute is valued and implemented. Good old Joe in shipping will become a hero when he implements that plan to improve productivity which he has been sitting on for the past 15 years.

- The overhead costs of running the business will be reduced. Workers will become more efficient. Increased profitability will result from tapping into the employees' minds as opposed to building more factories.

- Organizational structures will flatten, giving way to the formation of small, independent groups that act as support networks. Individuals will interface among groups to expand their expertise and knowledge.

- Personal and company goals will be achieved more often.

- New challenges will be met with enthusiasm and goals never thought of before will become a common way of life.

CHAPTER 2:

OWNERSHIP

IS A

VOCABULARY

FOR

SUCCESS

What do responsibility, authority and Ownership really mean?

What does empower mean?

WHAT DO RESPONSIBILITY, AUTHORITY AND OWNERSHIP REALLY MEAN?

As individuals within a society, we rely on our written and spoken language to guide and facilitate our interactions with one another. Yet, unfortunately, our language is seldom policed to maintain its intent and integrity. To fully understand Ownership, there are a few terms that cannot be interchanged.

Responsibility: The quality or state of being responsible, as moral, legal or mental accountability. Responsible: Liable to be called on to answer, liable to be called to account as the primary cause, motive or agent, being the cause or explanation, liable to legal review, or in case of fault to penalties, able to answer for one's conduct and obligations, able to choose for oneself between right and wrong.

Authority: A decision taken as a precedent. An individual cited or appealed to as an **Expert**. Power to influence or command thought, opinion or behavior. The official right to make a decision.

Ownership: Own; belonging to oneself or itself, for or by oneself, independent of assistance or control.

Take a minute and re-read these definitions. You'll see they're related. A person with authority has inherent responsibilities and Ownership of that for which they are responsible.

Unfortunately, in our everyday working world, *responsibility* and *authority* have been taken out of context. Companies and organizations routinely apply the words without reference to the meaning. They regularly outline areas of responsibility but seldom match it with the authority to do the job, causing grave consequences in the workplace.

Matching authority with responsibility is a valid business strategy that needs to be practiced. Companies need to become disciplined in using the words. Ownership is the solution. But it will take a re-thinking of how we structure companies, and most importantly, our *role* as individuals within them.

WHAT DOES EMPOWER MEAN?

Many books are currently being written for managers and executives that promote empowerment for workers. But "empower" means "to give official authority or legal power to." *These* books claim that workers need to be responsible for their jobs and solve the problems associated with doing the work. So managers are being advised to empower workers to take on more responsibility. What's new?

Workers have been responsible all along. Empowerment isn't truly being addressed because responsibility requires authority by definition.

Ownership is the true answer because it upholds that authority match responsibility. You can't do a good job if you can't make the decisions that affect your job. When you have authority, you're an **Expert** and you *own* the responsibility. Therefore, you're empowered.

Let's concentrate on the word Ownership, which pulls all these thoughts together into one very powerful message.

CHAPTER 3:

OWNERSHIP

IS A

PROBLEM

SOLVING

TOOL

How problems affect us.

How can we affect solutions?

All jobs can be viewed as a collection of problems or challenges that are solved by individuals. I only use the word "problem" for ease of understanding. Opportunities are just as much a part of the process. In order to succeed in our jobs, we need to know how best to handle problems or opportunities where they arise. Whether working individually or in a group, Ownership can be a powerful mind-set for solving problems, achieving goals and being more productive.

HOW PROBLEMS AFFECT US.

As human beings, we all encounter problems. A *problem* is a question or situation that presents uncertainty, perplexity or difficulty. The essence of a problem is that a person must discover what must be done in order to achieve some goal.

In our brains, a problem causes the lack of agreement or inconsistency between beliefs and actions. To understand this, consider the field of music. In music, this type of inconsistency is called dissonance, or a mingling of discordant sounds, a clashing musical interval. In our brains, that's what problems are: a clashing noise.

When faced with a problem, we're motivated to find a solution. We don't like problems and want them to go away as quickly as possible. They're bad music, and we want harmony, not dissonance, in our minds. Whatever the problem, it occupies our thoughts until we achieve some sort of solution, or deny the problem altogether. The bigger the problem, the more dissonance, the more discomfort it creates, and the more energy we exert in solving it.

On the positive side, the same can be said for goals we want to achieve. In essence, when we set a goal for ourselves, we create problems. We think about a future reality of owning a bigger car or weighing 20 pounds less. If that picture doesn't match today's reality, we have dissonance in our mind. The importance we place on the goal determines how much energy we devote to solving the conflict.

How can we affect solutions?

How we solve a problem depends on its size and complexity. A problem's size is defined by the number of alternatives that must be examined (and rejected) before finding the solution, or by the number of steps required to produce a solution. Problems vary from being very well-defined to vague and ill-defined, differ in the number of steps required for their solution, and pose various kinds of difficulties.

Problems are easier to solve when people are familiar with, and can draw upon, related solutions. In contrast, unusual ideas tend to occur later and relatively slowly. The most difficult solutions, however, are creative ones. That's because these solutions must be both unusual *and* practical. Since most unusual ideas are not practical, finding creative solutions is very time-consuming.

With enough practice, however, people can learn to solve any problem more creatively and effectively; even developing what is called expertise. An **Expert** can solve problems quickly because he doesn't need to re-invent the wheel. He uses past knowledge of similar problems. This in-depth knowledge allows him to spot creative ideas more quickly, as well. And there is a great benefit to being an expert. **Experts** are hard to replace. The more you position yourself as an **Expert**, the more indispensable you become as an employee.

Ownership in the workplace assigns **Experts** to company problems and goals. This means the person in charge of the solution will take less time coming up with a more creative idea, because he is the most familiar with past solutions, has the most in-depth knowledge of the current situation, and the authority to carry out what's needed.

CHAPTER 4:

OWNERSHIP

EXERCISES

YOUR

BRAIN

What is the brain and how does it work?

What is the reticular activating system?

How do we process thoughts?

In order to solve problems, we need to understand how our brain works, and that *we* have complete control of our thinking process. Solving problems and taking advantage of opportunities are up to us and how *we* think. Although the mind remains one of the most challenging mysteries in science, there is much that we *do* know. And the principles can help you improve your performance.

WHAT IS THE BRAIN AND HOW DOES IT WORK?

The human brain is a complex system with at least 15 billion (15,000,000,000) nerve cells that receive, store, retrieve, transform and transmit information. The cortex, or outer layer of your brain, contains most of the decision-making centers that influence what you do, feel and think.

Information from the outside world flows into your cortex through your eyes, ears, nose, tongue and skin. After receiving this incoming sensory information, your cortex checks its memory files, and decides what you should do, or think, or feel in a given situation.

Once your cortex has processed the input and decided on a response, it sends command messages along motor pathways to your body's muscles and glands, which tells them how to react. From a biological point of view, your brain manufactures thoughts and behaviors. Your brain has the processing power of over 15 million computers!

What is the Reticular Activating System (RAS)?

Each and every day, we're bombarded with information and input from the environment. If we tried to process all that we see, hear, touch, smell and taste, we would go crazy. There's just too much to handle.

Fortunately for us, our brains have a coping mechanism. A scientist by the name of H.W. Magoun and his colleagues at UCLA discovered what is known as the Reticular Activating System (RAS).

The RAS is a network of neurons in the brain stem involved in the transmission of sensory input to other parts of the brain. It's the gatekeeper of the information allowed into our brains for processing. In essence, it filters out the majority of information we encounter and lets in what *we've* decided is important to us. The RAS looks for input that represents either threats or opportunities.

Magoun's experiments, which demonstrated the function of the RAS, involved animal subjects. An electrode was implanted in the RAS of a cat. The animal was allowed to continue its daily routine, but occasionally, a small amount of electrical current was delivered to the cat's RAS.

When the RAS was stimulated while the cat was awake, the

animal reacted as if it had "heard something." That is, it suddenly became tense and alert, as if its environment had suddenly changed dramatically and it ought to pay attention.

When the cat was asleep and short bursts of electrical energy were delivered to its RAS, the cat opened its eyes and jumped up, as if someone had stepped on its tail.

When the cat's RAS was surgically cut, it lapsed into deep sleep from which it seldom, if ever, recovered. If you shook the cat violently, it would wake up momentarily and move around for a minute or two. But, even if it were starving to death, it would soon lie down and drift off to sleep. They proved that sensory input was being received by the brain, but without the RAS associating any importance to it, the information was ignored.

Your own RAS functions much like the cat's. Recordings of brain activity taken from human volunteers suggest that informa-

tion from sensory receptors does indeed reach the brain during sleep. But falling asleep involves turning off the alarms of the outside world – that is, slowing down the activity in your RAS. As you drop off to sleep, part of your brain inhibits the firing rates of

neurons, or nerve cells, in your RAS so you won't be bothered except in real emergencies.

Since it sits atop your spinal cord and extends up into your lower brain centers, your RAS is in perfect position to act as a toll booth through which incoming sensory information must pass if it's to have an affect on your cortex. If the incoming message is trivial or routine, the RAS will allow your cortex to ignore the input. But if the message is viewed as important, the RAS alerts the higher centers of your brain, and they pay attention to the input.

As you read this book, your receptor cells are sending millions of messages per minute through to your brain. But your RAS is telling your cortex that it needn't bother with most of this sensory input. For instance, until you read this sentence, you probably were not consciously aware that your shoes and socks are full of feet, or that your clothes are pressing in on various parts of your skin. Your RAS has learned that these signals don't need your attention while you read. They're neither a threat nor an opportunity.

But a sudden change in the pattern of incoming information, as when a friend shouts at you, is recognized by the RAS as being important. It alerts your cortex that an emergency message is coming through. Your attention then shifts from vision (reading) to hearing (listening). The words your friend shouts at you are immediately processed by your cortex, and you respond appropriately to the emergency.[3]

Once we decide that something is important to us, discover a problem or set a goal, the RAS sends up antennae to look for helpful or informative input from the environment. This fact is important to the idea of Ownership in that **YOU CONTROL YOUR RAS**. If you decide to solve a problem or achieve a goal, your RAS will look for, and find, the information you need to succeed.

For an example of how this works, consider a mother and child. A mother can sleep undisturbed while a loud train goes by, an ambulance screams down the street, her husband snores or a host of other noises occur. But let her baby whimper in the next room and the mother jumps out of bed. Why is this so? The mother has decided that her baby's safety is important to her, and her RAS is tuned into looking for input that represents threats to her baby. When the RAS notices the slightest sound from the sleeping baby, the information gets through with a sense of urgency, and Mom jumps out of bed to check on the baby.

The same is true with opportunities. When we decide we want to achieve a goal, we create a conflict between current reality and where we want to be. Our RAS scans for information that could help us resolve the conflict. If we decide we want to buy a truck, all of a sudden we start noticing how many trucks are on the road. Then we notice all the car lots filled with shiny new trucks. Every time we pass a truck, it jumps out at us. They're all over the place. In fact, they were there the whole time. But, until it became important to us, we ignored the input. Our RAS filtered the information and we didn't even notice them.

At work, Ownership teaches us to use our RAS in order to become an expert, solve problems and achieve goals. As a first step, we need to fine tune our RAS in order to process information that will help us succeed.

HOW DO WE PROCESS THOUGHTS?

Lou Tice, an expert in the science of personal goal achievement, has done remarkable work in making the brain and its thought processes understandable. In Lou's "Investment In Excellence" cur-

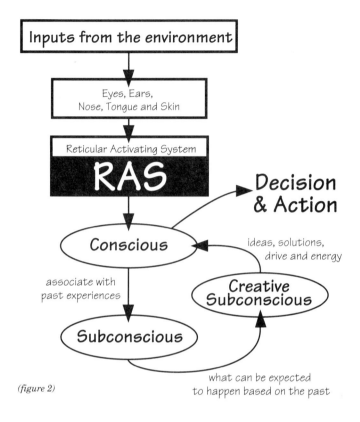

(figure 2)

riculum, his explanation of how the subconscious mind functions is as follows:

Once information gets through the RAS, it enters our conscious mind (figure 2).

From there, the information moves to the *subconscious* mind, which acts as storage for all our experiences and thoughts. Think of it as the hard drive in a computer. It keeps on file all of our experiences, thoughts and feelings. It's the level through which information passes on the way toward consciousness; an information store containing memories that are momentarily outside of our awareness, but can easily be brought into consciousness. Through hypnosis, people are able to recall early childhood experiences from the subconscious with amazing clarity.

The subconscious associates new information with past experiences. It asks the question, "Where have I seen this before?" and "What will happen based on similar past experiences?"

New information and associated experiences are then sent from the subconscious to the *creative* subconscious. The creative subconscious is the source of mental processes that lead to solutions, ideas, conceptualizations, artistic forms, theories or products that are unique and novel. The creative subconscious analyzes the data to see if we are heading for a positive or negative consequence. It comes up with, and creates, possible solutions on how to deal with previous associated consequences. The creative subconscious motivates us and creates energy through our thought process to solve the problem and take action.

Finally, the information and creative options are returned to our conscious mind, prioritized according to how much time and energy we need to spend on the information. We make a decision and take action. The thought process is completed.[4]

You probably never realized how much goes on in our heads every second of every day. Our brains never get a vacation, until we expire, that is.

Knowing how the brain works and how you process thoughts is critical to implementing Ownership as your new way of life in the workplace. The thought process produces decisions based on your experiences and the information received in your brain. Your RAS is the gateway of input to the cycle and you control your RAS. The quality of decisions you make will depend on how effective you are at fine-tuning your RAS to accomplish your goals.

CHAPTER 5:

ADJUST

YOUR

ATTITUDE

FOR

BETTER

PERFORMANCE

What are you saying when you "have to" do something?

What does it mean to "want to" do something?

Your attitude sets the stage for your performance. How we perceive situations can often have a positive or negative effect on the outcome, so when we set goals for ourselves or our companies, we have to be very careful how they're communicated. Ownership acts as a guide for your thought processes, keeping you on track toward the positive. And that's how goals are met.

WHAT ARE YOU SAYING WHEN YOU "HAVE TO" DO SOMETHING?

First, let's consider how a negative attitude affects our performance. When we view something as a *have to*, we're thinking that we *have to do something to keep something bad from happening to us.* For instance, we have to go to work or else we'll go broke, live on the streets, starve and live a miserable existence. Our thoughts are directed to avoid a negative consequence. The principle of action and reaction occurs, as well. If we think we *have to* do something, our very clever minds will concentrate on figuring out why we *don't* have to. For example, if I say to myself, "I have to get in better shape," I'll respond, "No I don't, I can't afford the time and besides, big is beautiful." Either way, the conflict is resolved in our mind; we removed the problem by convincing ourselves it really wasn't a problem.[5]

If you associate what you do with negative consequences, you'll do everything you can to get out of it. Negative thinking often means no performance at all.

WHAT DOES IT MEAN TO "WANT TO" DO SOMETHING?

Now, consider the positive attitude. If we look at a goal as something we want, our reticular activating system (RAS) will focus on finding information to help get us there. Whether we want to buy a truck, get a new job, improve sales by 20 percent, or improve quality, we'll tune into what can help us move toward our goal.

If the goal is seen as positive, *creative* energy is spent contemplating how to reach the reward. So, there's a much better chance that the goal will turn into reality. When you associate what you do with a positive result – when you *want to* – you'll also feel better about doing it. That's why Ownership preaches the need to "own" your goals. Achieving them will automatically become a "want to." As you incorporate Ownership into your thought process, you'll begin to shift much of what you do from *have to's* into *want to's*.

You'll begin to realize that there are positive results from your job and the work you do. The association you'll make between work and happiness will be positively linked. This is the first step in changing your attitude, blossoming into the solid performer you are and actually enjoying your work.

CHAPTER 6:

OWNERSHIP

STARTS

WITH

COMMON

SENSE

*Given the same input, people will
make the same decision.*

*There's more than one right way
to get something done.*

Every decision has a default decision.

Ownership is a tool that guides people and companies into making effective and efficient decisions. The theory is based on simple common sense: Given the same input, people will make the same decision; There's more than one right way to get something done; and Every decision has a default decision. Let's take a closer look at these ideas.

GIVEN THE SAME INPUT,
PEOPLE WILL MAKE THE SAME DECISION.

The American jury system is based on the assumption that a group of 12 people, when presented with the same information, will come to a unanimous conclusion. Let me demonstrate.

Imagine, if you will, that I am holding two markers, similar except one has a red cap and writes red, the other has a black cap and writes black. I ask a group of people what color will the red-capped pen write? Everyone in the group will say, "Red." Everyone has exactly the same information and thus will come to the same conclusion. A red cap must equal red ink.

Now, suppose half the group closes their eyes. I then switch caps on the markers. When I ask what color the red-capped pen will write this time, I get two different answers because half the group had different information. This very simplified example demonstrates how having the same information results in the same decision.

Today's world, however, is much more complicated. People have different backgrounds, experiences, education levels and attitudes that affect the information they receive. They bring unique sets of data stored in their subconscious and associate new information in different ways. This diversity leads to different decisions in the workplace. Ownership recognizes that the individual with the best information is the one closest to the work – the one who, in essence, keeps his eyes on the red and black markers at all times. For this reason, he needs to make the decision.

THERE'S MORE THAN ONE RIGHT WAY TO GET SOMETHING DONE.

It's often assumed that bosses or managers are the only ones with answers to problems. But the assumption is wrong. There's more than one way to solve a problem and more than one correct solution to a problem. As diverse as problems are, so are the available solutions. For 99 percent of the challenges we face, there's always more than one approach. Each solution is just as effective as the other.

If you're in New York City, for example, and have a meeting in

Boston, you have a problem. You need transportation to Boston. You can fly, drive, take a train or ride a bus. All options will get you there and solve the problem.

EVERY DECISION HAS A DEFAULT DECISION.

Not making a decision *is* also a decision. In Ownership, we refer to these as Default Decisions. The fact that a decision is not made has associated consequences.

Let's look at a true-life example (figure 3). Years ago I owned an old German car with well over 100,000 miles on the odometer. While driving one day, the red "brake indicator" light came on. Being the non-mechanic type, I panicked. Simple logic told me something was wrong with the brakes.

At that point, I was faced with a decision. Do I take the car in for repair? Sell it? Or hope that the light goes out and nothing happens? The decision to repair or sell the car is an active decision, to ignore it is the default. I chose to ignore it. Several minutes later, it went out, and I assumed the car had healed itself.

A couple weeks later, the light came on again. Once again, I was faced with a decision to fix, sell or let the default decision take effect. Again, I ignored it, and again the light went out. Continuing to drive the car, I hoped the problem was merely superficial and posed no real threat. However, anxiety overwhelmed me each time I hit the brakes.

Two more weeks passed when finally the light came on and

remained illuminated. By this time, the brakes screeched, the car shook and it became obvious I could no longer allow the default decision to take place. I was in a crisis management position. The car went in for repair.

News from the mechanic detailed a $1,500 bill for complete replacement of an extensively damaged sys-  tem. In my ignorance, I mentioned the light going on and off some time ago. As luck would have it, the mechanic informed me that if I'd brought the car in when the light first went on, he could have fixed the problem for $250. In my case, delaying the decision was a costly proposition. As with many problems, ignoring them and allowing the default decision only complicates the ultimate resolution.

This example illustrates several important points. Each situation has its own default decision. In most cases, the default

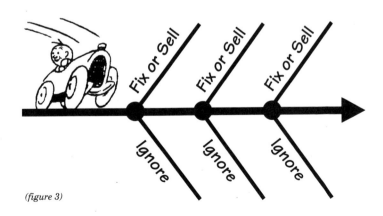

(figure 3)

decision includes more compounded consequences than an active decision made at the proper time. When the default decision prevails, it delays activity, reduces productivity and creates stress and tension that eventually leads to crisis management.

Ownership principles reduce the likelihood of default decisions by allowing the decision-making process to occur where it's most effective. Ownership places the decision-making responsibility with the person closest to the situation. That individual, if properly motivated, will have their RAS antennae looking for information to solve the problem. In the end, good decisions are made at the *right* time by the *right* people in the organization.

CHAPTER 7:

OWNERSHIP

IS THE

WORKPLACE

OF THE

FUTURE

Chaos = Unclear goals and heavy supervision

Visionary = Little or no supervision and no formal goals

Military = Specific goals and heavy supervision

The Owner Zone

Culture, by definition, is the human behavior that includes thought, speech, and action. It's dependent upon man's capacity for learning and transmitting knowledge to succeeding generations. The environments in which we do our jobs also have specific cultures. It is the behavior that is perpetuated in organizations. It's how things get done, and it impacts achieving goals. These work cultures are so powerful, they can either be beneficial or adversely affect our job performance. To understand how, let's look at the work culture matrix (figure 4). This matrix classifies organizations based on the existence of goals contrasted against the amount of supervision used to accomplish the work. You'll see why so many business organizations are down-sizing, right-sizing, and reengineering in order to change their cultures and move into what I call the Owner Zone.

WORK CULTURES MATRIX

(figure 4)

Chaos = Unclear goals and heavy supervision

A Chaos culture is an unfocused, frustrated working environment (figure 5). People are being supervised to death with no idea what the objective is. This results in unpredictable performance, high turnover and little productivity. Companies in this quadrant are doomed to fail.

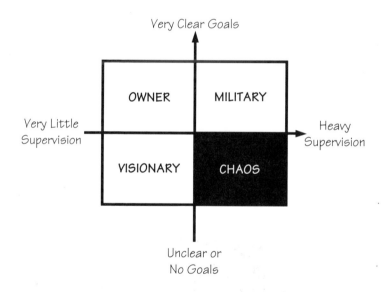

(figure 5)

VISIONARY = LITTLE OR NO SUPERVISION AND NO FORMAL GOALS

The Visionary culture is reflective of entrepreneurial or start-up company environments (figure 6). It's a *"Figure-it-out-for-yourself"* situation. It takes a unique individual to operate effectively in the Visionary Zone. People who are comfortable here include inventors, independent agents and entrepreneurs. Many company presidents and leaders prefer to operate in this zone as well. Others who want structure and direction will feel lost and abused if forced to work in the Visionary Zone.

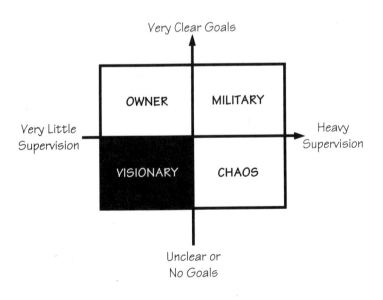

(figure 6)

MILITARY = SPECIFIC GOALS AND HEAVY SUPERVISION

The Military culture represents a highly controlled environment (figure 7). For the individual worker, it's a low-risk environment. If something goes wrong, someone else is to blame. Personal accountability is limited to the specific tasks, which are simple and well-defined. Many factory jobs and unskilled labor positions fall into this zone. These jobs are often replaced by automation.

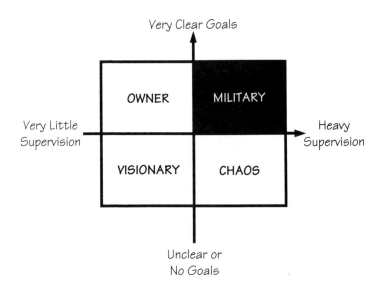

(figure 7)

Owner = Specific Goals with Limited Supervision

This is the Owner Zone (figure 8). It's what company environments should look like. In this zone, the goals and objectives are clear. The individual is responsible for performing tasks to achieve the overall goals with limited supervision. Most people are comfortable in this zone. They want knowledge of the goal and the freedom to achieve the goal in the way they see fit.

As you move counterclockwise from the Chaos to Visionary Zones, the salaries paid for those jobs increase. Jobs that operate in the Military Zone are lower paying and often replaced by automation as soon as it's economical to do so. The leaders of a company

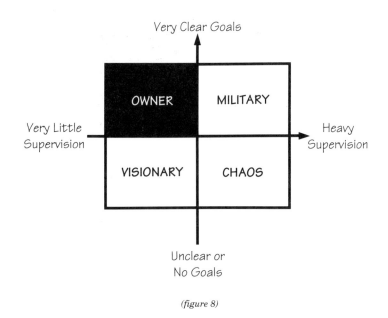

(figure 8)

often function in the Visionary Zone where it's up to them to define the goals. Most management positions operate in the Owner Zone, carrying out the direction set by company leaders. That's because people who work in the Owner Zone are viewed as **Experts**.

As we mentioned earlier, the word **Expert** is used in the formal definition of Authority. The term implies that a person who is considered an **Expert** is deserving of authority and responsibility. An **Expert** witness in our judicial system is the only type of witness that can provide an opinion that is considered valid for review by the jury. The more **Expert** you are in your job, the more valuable you become to companies in need of your expertise.

As you can see, work cultures can stand in the way of, or foster, our success. Ownership puts you in the winning corner by defining goals and letting people do *their jobs* with little supervision. It's the winning culture.

CHAPTER 8:

GET

WORK

DONE

MORE

EFFICIENTLY

WITH

OWNERSHIP

The established business

The start-up company

The common picture

The Ownership model

Companies get work done in many ways. Unfortunately, most of those ways are inefficient. That's because workers don't have a clear picture of their jobs tasks are duplicated and personal accountability is avoided. Ownership can help companies get more work done because it makes the workplace efficient, and puts people in charge of their jobs. To see how, let's examine some examples of how organizations get work done and introduce the Ownership model.

THE ESTABLISHED BUSINESS

Established companies often have most tasks assigned to specific jobs (figure 9). Notice that the authority (solid shapes) within the areas of responsibility don't match. Individuals are responsible for more than they have authority for. Sound familiar?

The area where tasks are unassigned or authority doesn't match responsibility is called the Default Zone. When a task in the Default Zone needs attention, seldom is anything done. The task is either unassigned or the responsible person hesitates deciding for lack of authority.

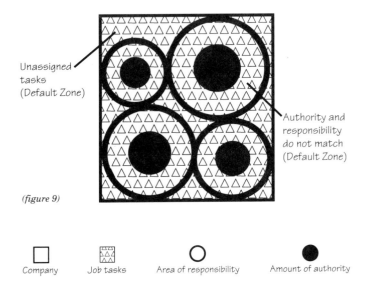

Unassigned tasks (Default Zone)

Authority and responsibility do not match (Default Zone)

(figure 9)

☐ Company   ▨ Job tasks   ◯ Area of responsibility   ⬤ Amount of authority

As we discussed earlier, Default Zone decisions are delayed until they reach a crisis point and force action. The Environmental Protection Agency is a great source of examples of unassigned tasks popping up in an organization. The EPA has the propensity to change regulations both quickly and retroactively. Keeping up with changes and current requirements is a major chore. Frequently, companies are caught without having filed a report or completed a specific test. When the citation is issued, the owner of the business quickly expands a specific job by assigning it the new task.

Figure 9 represents a company that has been in existence for many years. This type of company is characterized by a clear understanding of its business. Specific jobs are assigned a majority of necessary tasks, yet most of the jobs lack full authority for their level of responsibility. Workers typically function in the Military Zone. They know their jobs, are given specific direction, and are heavily supervised. When problems arise, the managers resolve them. Since the managers are aware of company goals and are able to choose methods of accomplishing them, only *they* function in the Owner Zone.

THE START-UP COMPANY

In the start-up company, there are numerous unassigned tasks and a large Default Zone (figure 10). Although jobs are given high degrees of authority, many tasks "fall through the cracks" and issues grow to crisis proportions. The boss assigns the task to a job only when the task is recognized. Much time is spent in a crisis management mode.

This scenario is typical of fast-growing or newly formed organizations. Workers and managers alike function in the Visionary

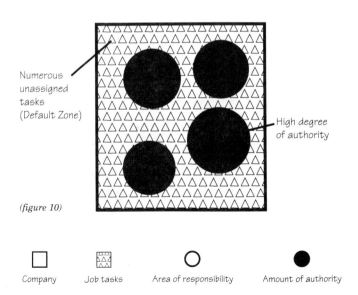

Numerous
unassigned
tasks
(Default Zone)

High degree
of authority

(figure 10)

☐ Company   ▨ Job tasks   ○ Area of responsibility   ● Amount of authority

Zone within an unstructured environment. Structure and procedures develop over time to help guide workers' efforts toward a common goal. Eventually, successful organizations transition to an Ownership environment. However, this transition takes exceptional management skill and is the major reason most new businesses fail.

THE COMMON PICTURE

In some cases, organizations have overlapping responsibilities (figure 11). Just about every task is assigned to multiple jobs and authority falls short of the responsibilities. This is a typical model of companies and government agencies, in particular.

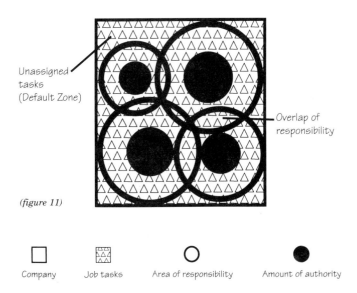

Unassigned tasks (Default Zone)

Overlap of responsibility

(figure 11)

☐	🔺	◯	⬤
Company	Job tasks	Area of responsibility	Amount of authority

For each task, there are multiple jobs responsible for the work, yet the jobs aren't given the authority to make decisions. By virtue of this, many decisions fall into the Default Zone and are left to grow into a crisis management situation.

The point is well illustrated when the Federal government gets involved in a hostage situation. Resolving the crisis typically involves the FBI, Secret Service, Bureau of Alcohol, Tobacco and Firearms, State Police and local law enforcement. Every agency claims jurisdiction in the case. Everyone is responsible for solving the problem, but who has the authority? Who's in charge? Oftentimes, the overlap in these situations makes for confusion and leads to devastating consequences.

THE OWNERSHIP MODEL

The Ownership model presents an ideal organization (figure 12). Nearly every task is assigned to a specific person with almost all the authority for the responsibilities. Certainly, new issues and tasks will arise, but once discovered, they will quickly be assigned to the proper person. Workers in this scenario function in the Owner Zone, with managers setting the company vision and future direction.

This is as close to a perfect picture of Ownership as you can expect. It's certainly a picture worth striving for. In time, more and more companies will structure themselves using the Ownership

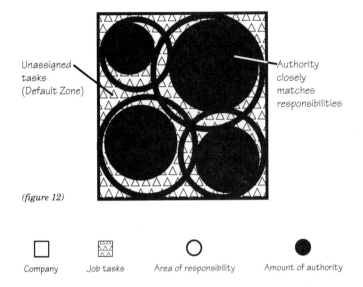

Unassigned tasks (Default Zone)

Authority closely matches responsibilities

(figure 12)

☐ Company   ▨ Job tasks   ○ Area of responsibility   ● Amount of authority

model and look for people who perform well in the Owner culture. The Ownership environment will fuel the performance of every employee.

CHAPTER 9:

HOW

MIS-APPLIED

RESPONSIBILITY

HOLDS

YOU

BACK

Responsibility without authority

Overlapping responsibilities

Political incubators

In order to become a superstar, you need Ownership. Unfortunately, certain situations inhibit your performance and the success of your company, including some of the environments we just described. Now let's focus on what else may be holding you back, in particular, responsibility without authority, overlapping responsibilities and the formation of political incubators.

RESPONSIBILITY WITHOUT AUTHORITY

One of the biggest blocks to job success is when you're responsible for a task without decision-making authority (figure 13). When problems arise, you may develop a solution to the problem, but it can't be implemented because you lack the authority. Problems then get ignored until a crisis arises. Adding to the frustration, you can be cited for poor performance because the problem exists within your area of responsibility. It is a catch-22 situation. You're damned if you do and damned if you don't.

When presented with a problem, your thought process automatically engages to get rid of the dissonance and solve the problem. Creative energy is exerted to come up with solutions, but they can't be implemented. The result is endless frustration.

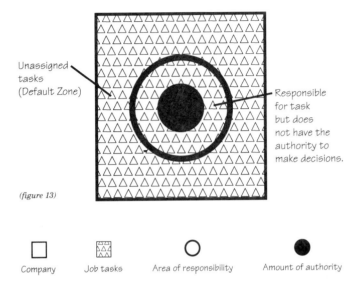

Unassigned tasks (Default Zone)

Responsible for task but does not have the authority to make decisions.

(figure 13)

Company   Job tasks   Area of responsibility   Amount of authority

Adding more fuel to the fire, the authority-holder (boss) often sees the issue as low-priority. A decision gets postponed or returned to the employee (still without authority). If the problem is solved, the boss is credited because, after all, she's the decision maker.

In this situation, the first step in solving the problem is to expand job authority to cover the task. Here's where personal accountability enters the picture. Understanding the problem is only the beginning. Once you, as a worker, identify a problem, **YOU** must take the initiative to bring it to management's attention. You may be thinking, "I've tried but they never listen." That may be so, but remember: Mind-sets are changing as more and more companies recognize the value of your expertise. Competition is also continually nipping away at your business, and that threatens your job.

To help you be more successful, here's a suggestion. Use your brain to identify work-related problems and generate creative solutions for them. Take the problem with several solutions to your boss. You'll find your boss surprisingly receptive to your ideas when you've

taken the time not only to identify problems, but also to solve them. It reduces the boss' workload and shows initiative on your part. Taking initiative will help you become an indispensable employee.

Remember, **YOU** are the driving force for change no matter what your job. **YOU** are the **Expert** in what you do and the best person to solve problems related to your job.

OVERLAPPING RESPONSIBILITIES

Another situation that may be holding you back is Overlap. Overlap is where the same task has been assigned to two individuals. In this case (figure 14) neither person has the authority to make the decision, so Default (or no decision at all) frequently occurs. One individual says, "I thought you were going to do it," and the other responds, "I thought you were." Obviously, the task doesn't get done, and it eventually grows into a crisis situation.

The boss informs the workers that they're both responsible for completing the task and to quickly resolve it. Frustrated and confused, they try to work out a resolution. If all goes well, agreement is reached and the problem subsides.

Let's consider an example. Keeping the floors clean in the factory may be the responsibility of both the production supervisor

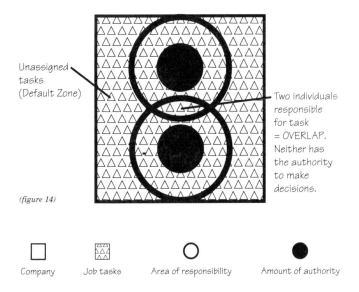

Unassigned tasks (Default Zone)

Two individuals responsible for task = OVERLAP. Neither has the authority to make decisions.

(figure 14)

□	⊡	○	●
Company	Job tasks	Area of responsibility	Amount of authority

and the maintenance supervisor. But without constant communication, there will be times when both think the other is doing the floors, and the task isn't completed. It becomes a crisis when the boss shows up and the floor is dirty. Both supervisors are then reminded of their responsibility. They go away and work out a schedule of who will clean the floors on what days, assigning their people the task. As long as the scheduled person shows up for work, the problem goes away.

From a company standpoint, the solution should have been to eliminate overlapping responsibilities. The task should have been assigned to one person and the authority expanded to cover the task. Cleaning floors needs to be assigned to one supervisor who can make sure the task is completed every day.

Why do overlapping responsibilities exist? We talked earlier about the value of jobs in companies. There's a direct relationship between authority and salary. If we imagine the big square in figure 14 to be a department instead of a company, the boss is paid the most money. More authority equals more responsibility equals more money. That's life. The boss (maintaining all of the authority) is paid on the ability of the department to perform the assigned work. Overlap is insurance. The boss goes home at the end of the day feeling good about taking care of her responsibilities. All of the work is assigned not once, but two or three times over. Like a good aircraft, backup systems are all over the place. If something happens, there are several individuals responsible and the chance of them all failing is remote. Someone is bound to take charge and get the work done. So, more often than not, overlap permeates the workforce.

In addition, the boss has the ultimate authority, so no decisions will be made without her approval. This builds in another layer of insurance against mistakes. It's also a time-tested method to identify who has the *talent to succeed*. Just throw them into the ring, and the one who survives and gets the work done will be the winner. The cream will rise to the top.

Believe it or not, management theory has supported this approach over the years, and many of you reading this right now are nodding your head in agreement. Many of us are working in this environment right now.

Overlap has one more important drawback. When companies are struggling and need to reduce costs, they begin to focus on areas of overlap. Overlapped responsibilities are then viewed as excess overhead. The company recognizes fault in paying two individuals to do the same task. Once identified, the company removes the overlap with a layoff and continues to perform the same amount of work with less people. Expenses are effectively reduced.

Initially, this is positive movement towards Ownership. If you've ever survived a layoff you know what I mean. In the short-term, things actually get better. There may be less people to do the work, but more work gets done. Productivity increases because the added workload on remaining individuals requires that they make more of the decisions, which is faster and more efficient.

Unfortunately, as business picks up, additional people are hired and the organization bloats to the pre-layoff condition. Unless management recognizes the need for permanent Ownership and abides by its principles, they'll retreat back to the comfort of overlap insurance.

Ownership encourages pro-active down-sizing by expanding job authority to match responsibility. Duplicate responsibilities simply don't exist. Overhead expenses are reduced to an efficient level.

POLITICAL INCUBATORS

Also detrimental to success in the workplace is the unproductive environment spawned from overlap, or what we call *political incubators*.

When overlap exists, the task is the responsibility of all individuals assigned it (figure 15). When a problem arises, each person invests time and energy to resolve the conflict. Each independently develops creative solutions to address the problem and remove the dissonance.

Political incubators resulting from overlap discourage teamwork. When you're in competition for authority, collaborative problem-solving becomes nearly impossible. Workers are busy promoting their own ideas and agendas in the hopes of increased authority, and ultimately, more income.

They may even engage in sabotage or other negative activities against co-workers. While caught up in their personal quests for

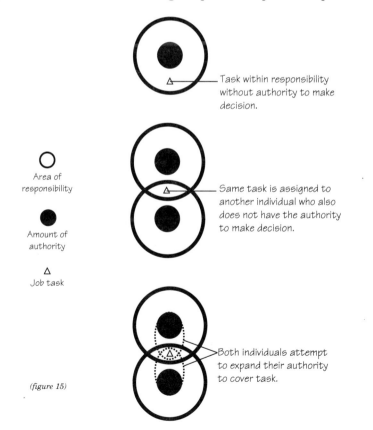

Task within responsibility without authority to make decision.

Area of responsibility

Amount of authority

△
Job task

Same task is assigned to another individual who also does not have the authority to make decision.

Both individuals attempt to expand their authority to cover task.

(figure 15)

increased value and income, workers lose sight of goals and company performance suffers.

When you have multiple overlaps, the problems are compounded. Multiple overlap areas lead to multiple default decisions, multiple political incubators and a hotly political resource wasteland.

On the other hand, with Ownership, there's no overlap of responsibilities and no competition for authority. Therefore, it encourages two or more people to work on problems and achieve effective solutions. Helping me is not going to hurt you. In essence, Ownership fosters teamwork.

Overlap is a dinosaur in the workplace. The performance insurance expected from overlapping responsibilities has never delivered. It's not the fault of the individual. Companies inadvertently motivate this destructive method of problem-solving. Nevertheless, the end result has been a frustrated workforce with high turnover, as well as wasted time, money, talent and energy. Ownership provides the tools to move forward to a more productive way of getting work done.

CHAPTER 10:

OWNERSHIP

IN

ACTION

Poorly applied Ownership

Properly applied Ownership

Building a house with Ownership

As powerful a tool as Ownership is, it cannot be instigated halfheartedly. You have to commit to all of its principles all of the time, or backsliding occurs. To avoid any early pitfalls, it's best to see Ownership in action, and point out early mistakes. Here are two examples that do just that: One in which Ownership is poorly applied and one which shows Ownership at its best.

POORLY APPLIED OWNERSHIP

Let's examine the customer service department at a manufacturing plant. When Ownership is not applied correctly, one situation that might occur is the holding back of authority. For instance, say the manager wants to review all the final paperwork details because he doesn't trust the accuracy of his customer service reps. The manager knows that he's ultimately responsible for the work of the department and, as insurance against mistakes, he has all orders go through him for approval. The customer service reps may hastily complete their paperwork, knowing that the manager always double checks the information and prefers to add the final details. Eventually, the reps will begin exerting minimal effort,

hastily completing their
paperwork because they know
the manager will double check
them anyway.

Over time, one result
would be a loss of confidence between the manager and rep. So later,
should an order placement problem occur, the individual closest to
the solution, the rep is more apt to ignore it and allows the default
decision to ensue. Solving problems is the job of the manager, the de-
cision-maker. When the problem becomes critical, the rep might be
inclined to offer recommendations, but recognizing that her input is
filtered, she's less motivated to come up with an effective solution.
In other words, she recognizes that the manager will ultimately
resolve the problem, so her creative subconscious mind assigns it a
lower priority. Her RAS, or brain filter, goes to sleep. She doesn't
have a problem, her manager does.

In this case, the manager has not granted all of the authority
and owns it himself. Until the boss transfers authority, the situation
will remain inefficient.

PROPERLY APPLIED OWNERSHIP

Ownership provides quite a different picture to the same scenario. With Ownership, the manager understands that the job of
entering orders correctly and completely is the rep's responsibility,
and so grants authority to the reps for decisions related to their

work. The manager rarely, if ever, double checks the orders. His role is to Coach. He monitors what's going on and keeps the goals of the department in clear focus for the reps. If a problem is uncovered, the order is turned back to the rep for correction. The manager doesn't solve the problem. Properly entering the orders then becomes a high priority for the rep.

When a problem develops, the rep's creative subconscious assigns it a higher priority, her RAS antennae (mind filter) scans the environment for information to solve the problem. She seeks input from management and co-workers and more creative energy is applied to finding a solution. Once the solution is identified, the rep makes the necessary decisions and implements the new idea. The rep doesn't forget the problem until she solves it.

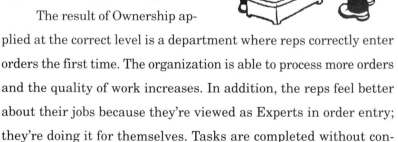

When the order has been turned in, the task is complete as opposed to a request for approval.

The result of Ownership applied at the correct level is a department where reps correctly enter orders the first time. The organization is able to process more orders and the quality of work increases. In addition, the reps feel better about their jobs because they're viewed as Experts in order entry; they're doing it for themselves. Tasks are completed without constant supervision and the company becomes a well-oiled machine.

Keep in mind that when people see that they're doing things for themselves, they're more likely to correctly complete tasks without constant supervision.

Building a house with Ownership

As you've read, Ownership can do wonders for a department. But what does properly applied Ownership look like company wide? Well, it's a lot like having a new house built (figure 16).

When having a house built, your first issue is to decide what amenities and living space you want. You develop a list of wants or goals to be included in the final structure. Now you need an architect and a builder.

If you have absolutely no clue about architecture or construction, you're at the mercy of the **Experts** you hire. This would be a

Building a House with Ownership

Homeowner

(figure 16)

 House   Tasks to complete house

pure example of Ownership because architects, general contractors and subcontractors typically run their own businesses.

The majority of tasks associated with building the house fall into either the architect's or general contractor's area of responsibility (figure 17). Unexpected issues such as special permits will come up along the way, so as the *owner* of the project, you either handle them yourself, or assign them to one of your **Experts**.

With the list of overall goals, the architect develops plans and blueprints for a suitable structure. She draws upon her experience and education to match your needs with sound building theories. It would be pointless for you to supervise the process because you

Building a House with Ownership

General Contractor

Painter

Electrician

Mason

Carpenter

Landscaper

Plumber

(figure 17)

 House  Tasks to complete house

know nothing about how the work is done. Your concern is the completion of the plan to your specifications. The architect has complete Ownership of developing the plans under the guidelines of your goals.

Once the plans are completed, you turn to the general contractor who goes about the task of building the house. Like most general contractors, he doesn't actually do the building, but rather, acts as the project manager and oversees the work of subcontractors to perform the multitude of tasks (figure 17).

Once again, it would be pointless for you to supervise the process of doing the work. Your involvement and concern is that the schedule is being met and that the building is being constructed to the architectural specs. Each subcontractor, under the management of the general contractor, has a specific set of tasks to complete. It's the responsibility of the general contractor to see that each subcontractor is scheduled to work at the proper time and that the structure is ready for the type of work to be performed.

In this example, there's no overlap. Each participant in the project is an **Expert** in their field, including the general contractor who's an **Expert** in the process of constructing homes. Painters don't wire structures and landscapers don't frame houses. They each *own* their jobs. Each subcontractor is also expected to be an **Expert** in their field. It's up to them to stay informed of new processes and materials and offer input to the general contractor on alternatives. The subcontractors also work together on ideas of how they can help one another.

The general contractor will also have a few tasks not assigned to a subcontractor, such as removing the scrap material or bringing in supplies, so he either does the work or assigns it. As you know, the items that aren't assigned often boil up into crisis situations. When a general contractor is involved, the blame goes directly to them. The better the contractor, the less unassigned tasks and potential for crisis management.

At long last, the project is completed and your dream home is a reality. Seldom does the process go without difficulty in some area, but in the case of construction, Ownership eliminates finger-pointing. Each task is identified, plans are drawn and specifications written to guide the process. When a problem comes up, the responsible **Expert** is quickly identified and they're accountable for solving it.

CHAPTER 11:

THE

PRINCIPLES

THAT

WILL

GUIDE

YOUR

SUCCESS

The boss is your Coach

Total commitment

Define the work

Remove overlapping responsibilities

Failure and mistakes lead to growth

Authority = Responsibility = Ownership

Work in the Owner Zone

Flexibility is critical

We've discussed the pitfalls of today's workplace and discussed the benefits of an Ownership environment. So, how do you make the transition into the Owner Zone? How do you own this wonderful thing called Ownership?

The principles of Ownership are the values and guidelines you'll need to incorporate the philosophy. They are the building blocks for your future in the workplace. They'll assist your thought process as you transition your work approach into the Owner Zone. When you live the principles of Ownership, you'll *own* it.

THE BOSS IS YOUR COACH

We've been talking about jobs within companies to give you a feel for the overall concepts. Now let's go a step further and look at how the concept of the boss fits in.

When a boss has responsibility for a number of tasks that are sub-divided into jobs, he owns making sure the work gets done. The individual workers own doing the work. It's an important point that needs to be understood.

The manager becomes your **Coach**. Just like coaches in athletics, he's not responsible for solving your problems. He's responsible for making sure you have the tools and knowledge to solve your own problems. The Coach then:

- Needs to know what's going on
- Sets the overall direction and relates how your job fits into the company vision
- Paints the picture of where the company is headed and helps you paint a picture that fits in
- Offers help without taking responsibility for your decisions
- Assesses your performance
- Channels your activities/tasks towards achieving the goals of the company

Imagine pouring a bag of marbles down a gutter. They'll bounce off the sides all the way down, but wind up in the same spot, the end of the gutter. The Coach acts like the gutter, guiding and directing your decisions, energy and activities. Without a Coach, it would be like throwing a bag of marbles onto a gym floor. Activities, decisions and energy would go all over the place and end up scattered.

Coaches are there to teach, motivate and guide you towards accomplishing the company goals. They're on the sideline monitoring activities, but you're the performer and the only one who can put points on the board.

Coaches focus your activities on movement toward the goal and make sure you stay on track. They assess performance and provide information related to the meaningful measurements. They're not there to solve the problems, but to provide the tools for you to solve them yourself.

Frequently, this means getting out of the way. I have a friend whose son played on a fourth grade basketball team. The Coach was very meticulous about how the kids performed. During each game, he required them to look over at the bench and get the play he wanted to run each time they had the ball. His desire to control their performance was obvious, but then again, he knew best how they should perform.

The team was winless going into the 6th game of a 10 game season. Their opponent was undefeated through the first five games. By the end of the first half, my friend's team was down by 12 points. With fourth graders, this is a huge margin to overcome against anybody, let alone the best team in the league. During halftime, the Coach was called away to take care of an urgent matter. He looked around and asked my friend's wife to help coach the second half. My friend's wife knew very little about coaching, but saw the need to help out.

A funny thing happened. The team won by 8 points under the new Coach. When everyone asked her how she did it, she replied, "I didn't know what to do, so I just told them to play." The players focused on the result, relaxed and performed. They believed in themselves and performed better than ever. As managers and coaches, you'll be amazed at what people can do when you let them.

Total commitment

Commitment begins with you. No matter if you're the janitor or the CEO, you need to look at how you do your job, recognize there's a better way, and commit to making a change. Ownership begins at the top of a company with a commitment to apply the principles. Ownership succeeds from the bottom with a commitment from every employee to actively participate. Your commitment will determine how successful you, and your company, will be.

Education:

Learning and fully understanding Ownership is critical. Everyone in the company needs to be educated on the concepts, principles and application of Ownership. You need to learn how to perform your job better than anyone on the planet. Take an avid interest in all aspects, both good and bad.

Model and reward:

Ownership needs to be modeled at all levels in your company. It's not just a matter of talking the talk as a manager; you also have to walk the walk. If you demonstrate Ownership, you'll succeed and people will follow.

In addition, when you're transitioning to an Ownership environment, there must be some form of reward for implementing and taking Ownership. Rewards motivate the type of activities and thinking you want. They'll acknowledge the type of behavior you want and speed the transition process.

Reward options are as unique as individuals: money, time off, plaques, certificates, vacations, lunches, dinners, whatever you decide. The point is to recognize someone for doing what's needed to live the vision. Recognition goes a long way, not only for the individual who receives it, but for everyone who sees what it took to get it. Make the activities you want a public affair.

Don't forget the Coaching staff. Remember, the success of your company is in your best interest. When you see that your Coach is implementing Ownership, find a way to recognize her efforts. Show her you appreciate what she's doing.

Ownership philosophy:

You need to develop your own personal philosophy about why you work. Your company needs a clear philosophy that's communicated to everyone, including principals, employees, customers, suppliers and the community in which you live. The **Ownership** principles need to be a key element of your and the company's philosophy.

Clear and defined goals:

Clearly defined goals need to be established within the framework of the Ownership philosophy. They exist to help make decisions. Goals set the necessary level of performance you need to achieve your vision and succeed. They are the stepping stones to realizing your vision.

Paint the pictures:

A *Vision* is a simple, focused and inspirational message about what the purpose of your work is. It paints a clear picture of a future reality.

Think of the vision as the company fight song, the rally cry for motivating and making sense of what you do. Business is a very simple concept. People buy products and services to solve problems. Successful companies identify problems people have and find creative ways to solve them. Companies then hire people to solve the problems of solving problems. The company vision is a shared picture of how you do that.

Based on what you know about the mind, once a vision is established, you've created a goal to work toward. The vision guides your thoughts and decision-making process. It adds meaning to your goals and keeps you focused on a daily basis.

Let's show you some good examples of company visions:

Federal Express:
Absolutely, Positively Overnight.

Short, concise and clear. There's no question what it means. It evokes emotion and helps guide every worker's decision-making process. Federal Express has grown to be one of the most successful companies in the world because of their commitment to their vision.

Federal Express employees have Ownership. Why else would an employee, working on a weekend in the computer room, go to the extreme of chartering a helicopter to fix a communications equipment problem on top of a mountain? It was an outrageous and very expensive way to solve the problem. That employee knew that if the equipment wasn't fixed, there was a good possibility the vision would suffer and some packages wouldn't get there "absolutely, positively overnight." That individual had the authority to fix what was potentially keeping the company from reaching their goals. In most companies, that sort of costly activity would result in at least a reprimand and possibly firing. In Federal Express, the individual was rewarded and recognized as a hero. Fed-X talks the talk and walks the walk.

A local car wash:

It may be your car, but it's our baby.

Everybody wants what they own to be well cared for. How better to communicate the desire to care for something than to relate it to your baby. This vision exudes emotion. What a great picture to paint for all the employees and customers.

Physio Control: *We save lives*.

Physio manufactures defibrillators (the things they thump you with when your heart stops). Their vision is a sharp and clear picture for everyone to keep in mind when making decisions. There's no misunderstanding the purpose of their work.

In addition to the company vision, you need to have a personal vision of how your work contributes to the bigger picture. As we discussed in the beginning, getting jobs is tougher than ever, so making your company succeed is definitely in your best interest. Your vision needs to inspire a *want to* attitude towards achieving the company goals. Together with your Coach, paint a clear picture of where you fit in.

For example, the janitor at Physio Control needs to see his personal vision as: I save lives by making the people who work at Physio feel good about their work areas. The Federal Express employee sees his role in the computer room as: I absolutely, positively must keep the computer system operating at all times, no matter what.

Measurement and feedback:

People want to win. We want to be a part of something bigger than ourselves. We want to contribute and to be a part of something successful. We want to know that what we do makes a difference. Winning motivates, and nobody says it better than the greatest coach of all, Vince Lombardi of the Green Bay Packers:

Winning is not a sometime thing; it's an all the time thing. You don't win once in a while; you don't do things right once in a while; you do them right all the time. Winning is a habit. Unfortunately, so is losing.

There is no room for second place. There is only one place in my game, and that's first place. I have finished second twice in my time at Green Bay, and I don't ever want to finish second again. There is a second place bowl game, but it is a game for losers played by losers. It is and always has been an American zeal to be first in anything we do, and to win, and to win, and to win.

Everytime a football player goes to ply his trade he's got to play from the ground up – from the soles of his feet right up to his head. Every inch of him has to play. Some guys play with their heads. That's O.K. You've got to be smart to be number one in any business. But more impor-

tantly, you've got to play with your heart, with every fiber of your body. If you're lucky enough to find a guy with a lot of head and a lot of heart, he's never going to come off the field second.

Running a football team is no different than running any other kind of organization – an army, a political party or a business. The principles are the same. The object is to win – to beat the other guy. Maybe that sounds hard or cruel. I don't think it is.

It is a reality of life that men are competitive and the most competitive games draw the most competitive men. That's why they are there – to compete. To know the rules and objectives when they get in the game. The object is to win fairly, squarely, by the rules – but to win.

And in truth, I've never known a man worth his salt who in the long run, deep down in his heart, didn't appreciate the grind, the discipline. There is something in good men that really yearns for discipline and the harsh reality of head-to-head combat.

I don't say these things because I believe in the "brute" nature of man or that men must be brutalized to be combative. I believe in God, and I believe in human decency. But I firmly believe that any man's finest hour – his greatest fulfillment to all he holds dear – is that moment when he has to work his heart out in a good cause and he's exhausted on the field of battle – victorious.

In order to win, you have to know how you're doing and adjust your activities as necessary. That's the reason sports are so popular. In sports, there's constant feedback on how the participants are doing. A golfer always knows her score. She knows how her performance is matching up to her expectations and what the goal is. In the end, it's crystal clear whether the actions and decisions made during competition were successful or not. The scoreboard tells the story and nobody argues with it.

Measurement and feedback add life to the picture. Feedback lets you know what behavior you need to repeat and focus on, and what not to repeat. The more you visualize how it should be done, the more your activities will move towards the vision. This is the process of fine-tuning your RAS antennae.

Whenever you provide feedback, word it so that the next time similar circumstances arise, the person associates what to do with a positive action. Discuss what you *want to* happen, not what you want to avoid. Instead of saying "don't run," say "next time, walk."

Feedback needs to go both ways. Your Coach needs to know how her performance is affecting you. The Coach plays a very important role in the success of your company. You can't afford to be afraid of letting her know how she's doing. We can all improve. In Ownership, everyone has an obligation to help those they work with and count on.

Football games are video taped to provide feedback and analysis of the team's performance. The camera is positioned high above the playing field so that everyone who's participating in the game is in view. This wide-angle approach provides feedback to the players on their individual performance, and illustrates the impact on the team's overall performance. During team meetings, the players and coaches watch the impact of their decisions and performance over and over and over again.

Successful coaches point out positive performance as the behavior they want, and need, to be successful. Mistakes are recognized, but the discussion centers around what needs to be done to turn the mistake into a success. Good Coaches don't spend a lot of time showing incorrect performance; it's not what they want.

You need to see how your job fits into the big picture and know how you're performing. In essence, companies, employees and managers all need to analyze their performance. The key is to measure what's important and what will lead you to your vision. What gets measured, gets improved. When you see what activities are making a positive impact on your performance, your RAS will fine tune itself and filter more input from the outside world to help you even more. Accurate and constant feedback are essential to producing results. The measurements you establish are the lifeline of feedback you need to be successful in the Owner environment.

Don't wait for someone else to do it for you. You're the **Expert**, you're the Owner. Take the initiative and determine what's critical to achieving your goals. Get the information you need and measure your performance constantly.

Your Job = Fix It:

An Owner's job is to find out what's holding back your performance and to fix it in order to reach company goals. You're the individual closest to your work. You're an **Expert** in what you do. You're the *ONLY* person who CAN FIX IT.

Step up:

Once a company makes a commitment to Ownership, it must begin to assign higher levels of authority throughout. Overlapping responsibilities must be removed. Individuals who fill positions must accept the authority that goes with the responsibility. Everyone must be held accountable for the performance of his/her job. There's nowhere to hide in an Ownership organization. Everyone is counted on to perform, no weak links allowed.

DEFINE THE WORK

Exactly what do you do? In most cases, it takes us a minute to think of how to answer this question. The reason is that our jobs encompass many activities. Most of the time, there are overlapping responsibilities with other jobs in the company, so answering the question is difficult.

In order to move forward with Ownership, you need to know what you do, what decisions you make and what your responsibilities are. When you buy a house, the deed is very specific about the exact location of the property and the structure. You won't see language like "It's up on the north side of town and is kind of big." The exact coordinates of where it's located in the county, the total square footage, number of floors, bedrooms, and even a picture of the house, are included to eliminate any chance of misunderstanding what you own.

The tasks associated with doing the work of the organization need to be broken down to the "deed" level. The more exact the wording is about what you own, the less chance of misunderstanding. For example, one task may be to order office supplies. This would be broken down to include taking inventory of supplies, filling out order sheets, calling suppliers, mailing or calling in the order, filling out the requisition, and so forth. The idea is to identify each and every task necessary to accomplish the work.

Identify decisions:

All of the decisions necessary to perform each job need to be identified. You make thousands of decisions every day without realizing it. Ownership is the vehicle for having the *right* people make the *right* decisions at the *right* time in order to accomplish goals.

As you begin the process of identifying who owns what, and who should make which decisions, you'll quickly notice varying degrees of decisions. We talked earlier about how owning something doesn't always mean complete and unconditional control. The same concept applies to decision-making in Ownership. Some decisions

within your area of responsibility will require your
Coach's involvement. Notice
that we said, "Coach's *involve-
ment.*" The boss *will not* make
the decision, that's not Ownership. You have the responsibility,
authority and Ownership; the Coach assists the process. This is a
very important concept to understand.

Let's discuss two categories of decisions that will clarify this
process. Keep in mind that many decisions fall into a gray area and
handling them takes teamwork with your Coach. We'll label the two
discussion categories, Toothbrushes and Renovations.

Toothbrushes:

Toothbrush decisions relate to your job, only your job and
impact no other group or individual. You have complete control of
deciding how to deal with the decision (figure 18). When you own a
toothbrush, you can replace it, modify it or throw it away; it's completely under your control. These decisions, for the most part, are
simple in nature and basic to your work. Whether you use a blue
pen, black pen or marker to fill out a form is an example of a toothbrush decision.

Warning! Don't take toothbrush decisions lightly. You'll be
surprised how significant they can be. I was working with a grocery
store produce department on implementing Ownership and learned
a very important lesson.

After training the manager and assistant on the fundamentals
of Ownership, they were hooked. They wanted my help in getting

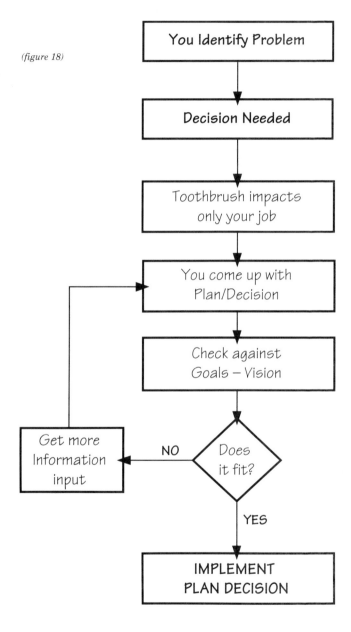

(figure 18)

Toothbrush decisions are simple in nature and affect only your job. It's up to you to identify problems, gather information and make decisions that fit with the goals of the company.

Ownership in their department. I met with the entire produce crew and reviewed the principles of Ownership. I asked what specific issues needed to be addressed in the department.

"Rubber bands, man, rubber bands," said one of the guys. Obviously, elaboration was needed. The night crew was responsible for restocking the produce area for the next day's business. The task is straight forward. Once a crew member understood the process, they functioned unsupervised. The night crew started at 4:00 P.M. and the assistant would spend an hour going over the night shift's objectives before ending his own shift.

Part of the night crew's responsibility included setting up the broccoli display. It's a simple job. You go to the back, find the case of broccoli, sort for acceptable quality heads and set them in the display area until it's restocked. Many of the heads were small, so they would combine two or more with a rubber band to create a unified size for shoppers.

The store took pride in having the town's best selection of quality produce. In fact, it based a major marketing campaign on it. The options of setting out inconsistent broccoli or under stocking the display were unacceptable.

All produce supplies were ordered by the manager or assistant because they were in charge of the purse strings. More often than not, neither paid attention to see if there were enough rubber bands. It was the responsibility of management to order them, but such an insignificant issue was overlooked until the crisis point.

When they ran out of rubber bands during the restocking, the night crew had no choice but to move on to the rest of their work. In the morning, the manager and assistant would find an unacceptable restocking job. The night crew would leave a note explaining why they left the broccoli section short and request the assistant to get rubber bands. It was a crisis, and everybody pointed the finger.

The assistant would place an order for more rubber bands and get an intermediate supply from another store. The produce department would have a day with less broccoli available for their shoppers. Consistency and quality were the hallmarks for this company, and when the department didn't look picture perfect in the morning, the department failed. It was serious and frustrating. Unfortunately, the same scenario came up every time they ran out of rubber bands. Since the assistant was responsible for ordering, he had ownership of the task. The night crew was responsible for using the rubber bands, but had no authority to make sure they were available.

When we were meeting and discussing Ownership, the problem was brought to our attention. One of the guys made the following comment, "We're the ones responsible for stocking the broccoli, why not give us Ownership for ordering the rubber bands and let us decide when we need more? We know when we're running low, and we'll make sure they're always there."

The light bulbs were flashing. The assistant and manager both looked at each other and said, "What a great idea. Consider it done. You guys now own the rubber bands and have the authority to order them whenever necessary." One by one, you could feel the power of Ownership restoring peace to their jobs. What seemed like a major stumbling block became a moot point. A lingering problem and source of frustration over a toothbrush-type decision was addressed and eliminated in the span of five minutes.

The lesson here? Don't take the minor decisions for granted. Keep a lookout for who should be ordering the rubber bands in your company.

Renovations:

Unlike toothbrush decisions, renovation decisions are those that impact others in your group or company. Your Coach needs to be involved with renovation decisions. The level of involvement changes over time as the Ownership expertise and trust grows between you and your coach.

Once again, we said the Coach is *involved*. We did not say that the boss makes the decision. It's yours, and you own it. Remember, your Coach is ultimately responsible that the work gets done and goals are achieved. His role is to guide the marbles down the gutter to achieve the goal. Not allowing you to cause a company catastrophe is what he owns.

Therefore, when your decision will impact others, you need to review it with your Coach (figure 19). The Coach's role is one of checks and balances to insure activities stay on track. The Coach is there to help. In order to fulfill his role, he must stay informed of what you're doing, and channel the energy and decisions which impact other areas of the company.

For example, you may see an opportunity to increase sales by using a new and innovative method of advertising. Suppose your idea shows some promise, but is very expensive. In this case, spending the money on advertising may eliminate other options to increase sales. It's up to you to learn who will be impacted should the plan fail and identify recovery plans. You're accountable for the

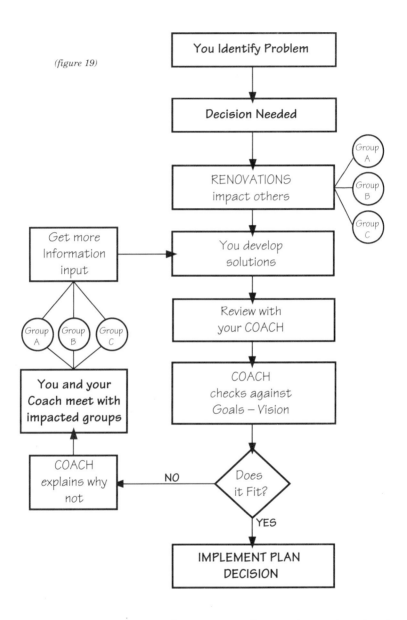

(figure 19)

Renovation decisions impact other groups in the company and need to be thoroughly evaluated prior to moving forward. The Coach is a resource to assist you in gathering the best information for you to develop an effective solution.

results, good or bad.

Should your boss recognize that your plan does not fit with the overall goals, it is his responsibility to explain why not. The two of you meet with the groups that will be impacted by your  decision in order to gather more information and refine your plan. However, *you control the process until it is completed and a workable solution is in place.*

In the early stages of implementing Ownership, the Coach will be involved in many more of your decisions. When your mutual level of confidence and trust grows, the involvement will decrease. In the long run, your Coach doesn't concern herself with your toothbrushes nearly as much as with the renovations and how they impact the team. You both need to learn the difference and be disciplined in identifying which category decisions belong.

This process puts the authority in your area of responsibility and, at the same time, keeps the Coach updated, informed and able to do his job of guiding marbles. Everyone effectively stays on track and in tune with one another.

REMOVE OVERLAPPING RESPONSIBILITIES

Another principle of Ownership that must be followed for success is to remove the safety nets. Pro-actively restructure the work you do. Make it clear that if a job doesn't get done by the owner, it doesn't get done and impacts the entire team.

Everybody knows who's who:

Authority levels, responsibilities and job definitions should be clearly understood and communicated throughout the company. Everybody needs to know who does what. As a result, you become aware of other **Experts** and where help is when you need it. That's why Ownership requires workers to see their jobs in a larger perspective. They need to understand how their jobs impact other jobs within the company.

You hold the deed:

Only Owners can transfer Ownership. If you decide to make someone responsible for part of what you own, you must pass along the authority.

Jobs are defined by what people own:

When you have Ownership, the role you play is often more encompassing than traditional job descriptions. As an Owner, your role is to define your contribution. This takes re-thinking about job descriptions.

We talked earlier about customer service and quality being part of your philosophy and vision. You need to break down what you do in relation to achieving your quality and customer service goals. For example, if you're in sales, what do you own? Some of what you own may include courting potential customers. Everything involved in accomplishing that objective is yours, including: sales calls, factory visits, preparing proposals, convincing customers to do business with your company. You own them. Others will be involved in the process, but you own *getting new customers to the point of paying for the products and services your company offers.* The decisions you make on how to do this need to fall within the philosophy and vision of your company.

Let's look at another example. If you're in customer service, what do you own? It may include: taking orders from customers and notifying your factory, communicating schedules to the customer, arranging for proper delivery, notifying the customer in the event of a late delivery, or notifying the factory in the event of a requested schedule change. Others are involved in the process of making the product available for delivery, but you own *the communication between your customer and your factory.* Your decisions are guided by the company philosophy and vision.

Now let's consider Ownership when you're the production person. What do you own? Imagine it's a very small company and you're the only one who builds the product. In this case, you own *meeting or exceeding the performance expectations for the final product.* In the process of building the parts, you own how it gets done. Your decisions are also guided by the company philosophy and vision.

Owners are experts:

In order to be successful and contribute to your company, you need to become an **Expert**. If you're the mail room clerk, become an **Expert** in shipping and package distribution. If you're a receptionist, become an **Expert** in that area. You need to be the best at whatever your job is, better than anyone on the planet.

Just keep in mind that you don't have the luxury of working for a company that doesn't have competition. I'm sure you seldom think of it, but how good is the person who works for your competitor doing their job? Are they more **Expert** in what they do than you? And if so, is that enough of a difference to make your customers do business with them?

Don't believe it's only the sales people who represent the company image to customers. If you're the receptionist and someone calls, you *are* the company on that phone line. If you're the shipping clerk, you're the last link of your company's product to your customer. If you throw the product sloppily into a box, you're sending a very real message about your company to your customer. If your work area is a mess when a customer comes to visit, you're influencing them negatively. Would your customer want to work in an environment like yours? If the people working for your competition are doing a little extra, taking the initiative to make their companies better, and you're not, it could mean the difference between you or them looking for a job.

Competitors are real, they exist. They're people just like you and me. They have families and houses and cars and wants and needs. They work to satisfy those needs. They want the same things you do. When a competitor gets business from your customer, they're taking money, security and happiness away from you. They "pillage your village." Stop and think for a minute. Do they practice Ownership? Do they have what it takes to succeed tomorrow? Can you afford to gamble that they don't? Don't let them get the edge. You become the absolute best at whatever you do. You'll become more of a contributor to your company and help secure your own future in the process.

FAILURE AND MISTAKES LEAD TO GROWTH

Playing it safe results in mediocre performance. Risking launches success. Thomas Edison failed 2,500 times to invent the light bulb before he succeeded. Abraham Lincoln lost 6 elections for public office before being elected President. Where would we be today if people didn't try again after failing? Trying is the first step to winning.

Remember: how you think affects your success. If two people analyze the same information and one associates the new information with a past failure while the other associates it with success, who do you think is going to achieve the most?

Failure is first anticipated, then realized. So is success. If the person making the decision (owner) believes the action is related to success, he'll work towards that picture. Remembering how the brain works, his RAS will tune into inputs that will move him towards his goal.

Failure and mistakes need to be tolerated and encouraged, provided:

- The same mistake is not repeated.

- The activities and decisions made were part of a well thought-out approach to solving a problem.

- Everyone learns from the process. The scenario is recognized, reviewed and analyzed in a non-threatening way so others may benefit from the investment.

Failures and mistakes are great learning opportunities, if you take the time and have the courage to make them positive (figure 20). When dealing with mistakes, the complete organization's commitment must be rock solid and the threshold of pain extended. Just like any team, you don't give up when a player fumbles the ball, nor do you take them out of the game. You react by teaching the skills necessary to succeed and exercise patience with the process. The most important thing is to praise in public and criticize in private. When reviewing a mistake in public, it must be done in a non-

personal manner. Respect for the individual is paramount to Ownership.

Remember, organizations are designed to eliminate mistakes and managers are conditioned to insure against it. Changing your work culture will take time. Overlap is an unacceptable alternative. Dealing with a little transitional pain is to be expected. The pain will be worth it. Success in the face of failure is powerful. The Owner gains confidence in himself, the Coach develops improved management skills, and trust builds between Coach and worker. A positive step is taken towards the company goals. The process of Ownership is proven once again.

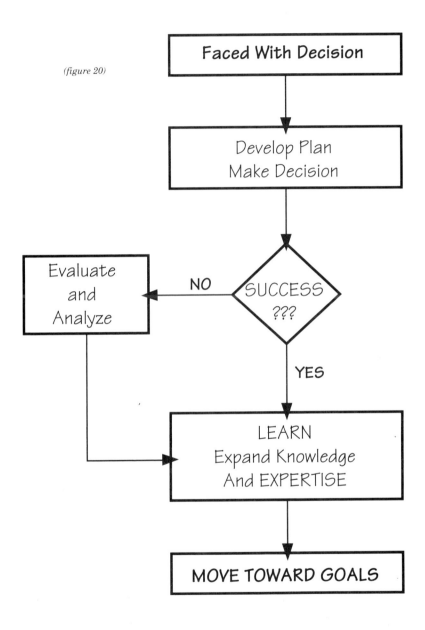

(figure 20)

Capturing the value of mistakes requires having the courage to review them for the learning investment they are.

AUTHORITY = RESPONSIBILITY = OWNERSHIP

Any questions?

Ownership replaces the words responsibility and authority. This is a vocabulary issue. The words we use to communicate with one another are very important. The associations you develop with certain words motivate certain behavior. **Ownership** encompasses all of what we need to do in our jobs and companies. Use the word.

WORK IN THE OWNER ZONE

Ownership becomes the culture of the company. They, them and theirs becomes we, us, ours, me and mine. *Want to's* replace *have to's*. Whatever zone you're in today, you need to get comfortable working with goals and little supervision. You need to be disciplined in pursuing the end result without constant direction.

FLEXIBILITY IS CRITICAL

Fine-tuning is critical. As Ownership unfolds, there will be many questions and issues to address. Work assignments and decision making will need to be adjusted until the most effective fit is accomplished. Some individuals are more skilled in certain areas. How work is done must be flexible enough to take advantage of individual expertise. In the beginning, there will be much trial and error.

Don't be disappointed if things are a little bumpy at first. Keep in mind that you're headed to a much more wonderful place to spend time working. The rewards will far outweigh the pain of getting there.

CHAPTER 12:

OWNERSHIP

IS

AN

ADVENTURE

The agony of managers

Business as usual

Don't stop now

The leap into Ownership

LET GO of the bicycle seat

Workers step up

YOU are the driver

Hang in there

Ownership is an exciting experience filled with challenges. It is truly an adventure. Like any adventure, there will be ups and downs during the transition process. The reason: at the concept's core is the tolerance for mistakes. You can count on them. People who never made decisions before will now be required to do so. Authority levels will increase to cover responsibilities, and as accountability shifts, mistakes will happen.

In order to succeed, commitment from the top is critical. When you embark on the Ownership adventure with your eyes wide open and a commitment to persevere, how you handle the initial stumbles will set the stage for the success or failure of the entire program.

People need to see it's okay to make mistakes, that they won't get shot or fired for stumbling. Eventually, everyone's anxiety will subside, and you'll move along faster.

THE AGONY OF MANAGERS

The majority of transitional pain will be felt by the management team (Coaching staff). After all, their role is changing radically. It's going to take a lot of courage to implement Ownership, and I commend you for doing so. Don't worry that people keep making bad decisions. There's a major difference in motivation when an employee owns his job because bad decisions reflect directly on him. It hurts his pride which motivates him to make corrections. That's human nature. He wants to look good because there's no one else to blame. And that will keep bad decisions from happening too often.

BUSINESS AS USUAL

In the beginning, the company should set goals and performance expectations consistent with its established philosophy. These are then handed over to the management team and broken down for individual groups. Each manager will have a set of tasks to be completed by his group like a contractor has tasks for his subcontractors. Unlike building a house, however, most workers aren't subcontractors. They don't run their own business. Operating in an Ownership environment will be foreign to them. Most likely they will be transitioning from a military environment where accountability has been very low. So be patient with the learning process.

During this time, it's the managers who will be held accountable for ensuring that work is adequately completed to accomplish goals.

Managers' expectations should be clearly defined and communicated (figure 21).

For example, say a company sets a goal to increase sales by 20 percent. The sales manager puts together a plan that details where the new orders will come from. She outlines on whom the sales-people will call, how often they will call, how they will conduct the

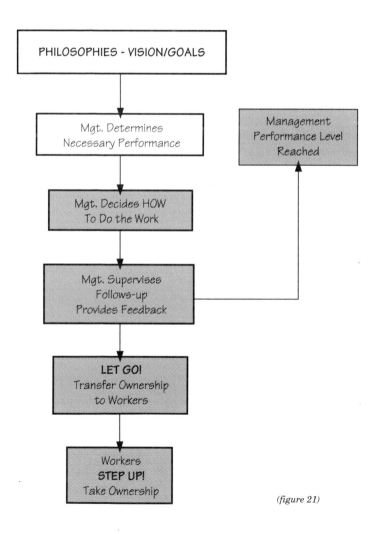

(figure 21)

call, what products will be demonstrated, and so on (figure 22). The plan to reach the goal is very specific. It's a recipe to reach the target. This plan also provides the meaningful measurements needed in order to track performance.

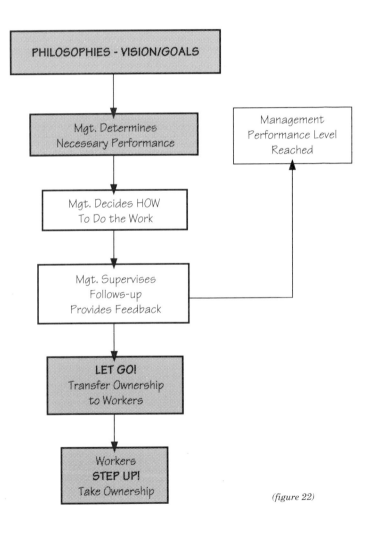

(figure 22)

The employee then makes the sales calls, demonstrates products and provides feedback to the Coach, who follows up and adjusts efforts as needed. This feedback loop continues until the operation is running smoothly and everyone knows what's required to achieve the Coach's goals.

Up until now, the Coach has made all of the decisions about how the work is done and is monitoring, double checking and overseeing the work. When problems come up, she fixes them. The manager is initiating the follow-up and feedback loop to insure all is going well and making adjustments as needed.

By now, Ownership is finally starting to take shape. The goals of the organization have been established within the context of the company's philosophy. They're broken down and communicated throughout the organization. The Coach for each department has figured out a way to reach the goal and is closely monitoring to see that it's happening. The organization is up and running. Performance is moving toward the goal. Now is time for the next big step.

THE LEAP INTO OWNERSHIP

To complete Ownership, it's time to transfer Ownership to the workers, and for the workers to step up and take it (figure 23).

The Coaches have to let go of the decision-making process and transfer the authority to the workers. What's been held closely by the Coach now belongs to the workers! The boss starts coaching but the workers own the job. It's up to them to figure out what customers to call on, how to call on them and what products to demonstrate, in order to reach the 20 percent sales increase.

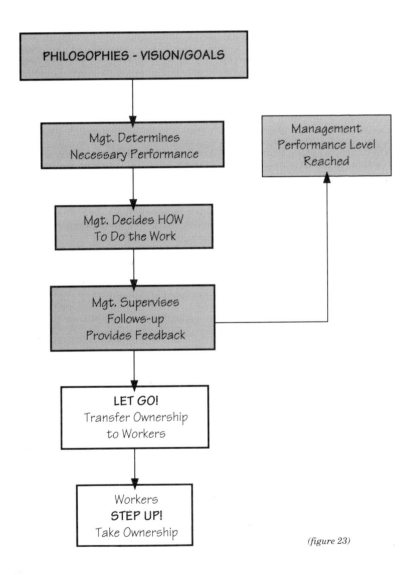

(figure 23)

DON'T STOP NOW

This is where most companies make a mistake. They stop – "they" being the executives. But if they stop before transferring final ownership to the people who do the job, the workers will recognize the lack of commitment and put their brains on hold. They go into a comatose, zombie-like state. Just like the cat which has its RAS severed, they switch off their antennae and drift into "la la land." And why not? If the bosses aren't going to release the reigns, if the Coach is going to fix all the problems, the workers can go back to behaving like renters instead of Owners. The initial foundation for Ownership will crumble and all the hard work will be wasted.

LET GO OF THE BICYCLE SEAT

To really understand the importance of letting go of authority, consider the analogy of a parent teaching a child to ride a bicycle. Up until children learn to ride their bikes, their worlds are very limited. Areas outside the house and yard are foreign territory. At a certain age, children begin to get interested in expanding their horizons but are limited to a small area within walking distance, or eyesight, of the ever-present parent.

The prospect of being able to transport themselves without the overshadowing assistance of another is intoxicating. They see the bicycle as a means to break free of this entrapped world.

The first step is to purchase a bike and attach training wheels. Riding the bike with the security of the training wheels is comforting. It's short-lived, however, because all the other kids are riding without training wheels, and they *want to* be like the others. The greater the want, the quicker children learn to ride.

The anxiety of both children and parents is extremely high the day the training wheels are removed. Sure, there's the precaution of a helmet, but at some point, the parent running alongside holding the bicycle seat will have to **LET GO**. And letting go can mean their child will fall down and crash, even get bumped, bruised and bloodied in the process. This is very hard for parents to endure because of their role to protect children. Here they're voluntarily putting them into a dangerous situation.

Now, if you were the parent teaching your loved one to ride a bike, you wouldn't cancel the process if she failed. You wouldn't pick up the bike and say, "That's it, you tried and failed. We're putting the bike away forever." No, you pick up your child, brush her off and put her back on the bike to try again. You can't keep her from failing. She has to learn it for herself. You're the Coach.

She may fail time and time again, but you keep working with her until, at that magic moment, she takes off, balances herself and rides off all by herself. It's a tremendous achievement for you and your child. Your child now has a whole new world opened up to her.

For parents, the joy of seeing their child overcome such a challenge is unparalleled.

WORKERS STEP UP

Ownership requires more than management stepping up to the plate. It's not a one-way street. Workers have to step up and take Ownership too. For the transfer to take place successfully, here's the mind-set employees must have:

- I understand what my job is.

- I understand how to do it.

- I'm an Expert in my job.

- I understand the company goals and have a clear picture of where we're headed.

- I know what the company philosophy is, and I will use it to direct my decision making.

- I want to take control of the decisions in my job. I see how it will benefit me and help me achieve my personal goals.

- I know when I get Ownership, I'll be on my own, but that my co-workers and Coaches will be there to help when I need it.

- It's okay if I make a mistake. I'll learn and increase my knowledge as a result.

- I'm ready for Ownership.

- I want Ownership.

When you're thinking like this, the motivation is there. Your RAS will be operating at full power to achieve the goals of the company. It's time for the Coaches to **LET GO!**

You are the Driver

Once the Ownership (real authority for decisions) is transferred, the follow-up/feedback loop becomes worker-initiated. Now that you're responsible and accountable, you need to look for input to stay on track. Wake up, flick-on the switch and activate your brain's RAS. Make it your priority to find ideas and input that will help your performance because the safety net is gone. Take action to protect and improve what you own.

Keep in mind that authority abused is soon lost. Authority is not a free ticket to do as you please. It's a tool to be used in performing your job so as to achieve the goals of your company. Abused authority results not only in the loss of authority, but also in the loss of responsibility, income, and possibly your job. You need to respect the responsibility of having authority.

Hang in There

The same steps take place when transferring Ownership. There will be mistakes and set-backs. The key to success, however, is to continue allowing mistakes and to ride them out as long as they're not devastating to the operation.

Bob the Muffin Man:

My favorite example of Ownership in action occurred when I was implementing the Ownership principles in a large grocery chain. Seeking to improve operations through Ownership, management and I chose to experiment with one store. We picked a location filled with controlling managers and Military Zone employees.

To thoroughly test the principles, the store manager selected the bakery department as the starting point. This posed an extreme challenge as the head baker was a disgruntled employee and marginal performer. The experiment was basically executed as a last-ditch effort to salvage the bakery and head baker's job.

After educating the staff with a series of Ownership seminars, I got to work. Sitting down with the baker, who's name was Bob, I asked, "If you owned this bakery, Bob, how would you do things differently?" The ideas came screaming out! For the next 90 minutes I took notes. Amazingly, Bob had never been asked for input.

After meeting with Bob, I met with the store manager. He reviewed my notes and was intrigued by Bob's idea to expand the bakery's muffin line. Bob felt the store offered too few varieties at too low a price (believe it or not).

Seeing a tremendous opportunity, the store manager and I gave Bob total control of the bakery's muffin products. With no strings attached, Bob was given complete Ownership.

In less than a month, the store went from three varieties of muffins to thirty-two. The price went up by 40 percent, and sales increased by a factor of five. In two months the bakery was supplying local hotels and restaurants, and working around the clock to meet demand.

Throughout the chain, Bob became known as "Bob the Muffin Man." He was revered as the muffin **Expert**. His attitude changed as well; he now beamed confidence and pride. It was no surprise when he became a leading company contributor.

Sales increased and a marginal performer became a superstar simply by asking the question, "How would you change your job if you were the owner?" Needless to say, Ownership took hold throughout the company. Today, the grocery chain continues to succeed and grow using the Ownership principles as the guide for their organization.

CHAPTER 13:

OWNERSHIP

UNLEASHES

YOUR

PERFORMANCE

After the difficult, final stage of **LETTING GO** is complete, exceptional results will be enjoyed.

Inevitably, and almost categorically, job performance will exceed the levels established by the Coach. Solutions never thought of before will be implemented, making the business more efficient. **Experts** throughout the company will be driving the performance (figure 24).

You'll begin to see marginal and non-performers blossom into exceptional employees all over the company, simply due to the fact that Coaches have let go of control and gotten out of the way. Soon the workers will eclipse goals set by management and establish a new performance level for the company. They'll see themselves as superstars! And they'll be motivated, even addicted, to doing better.

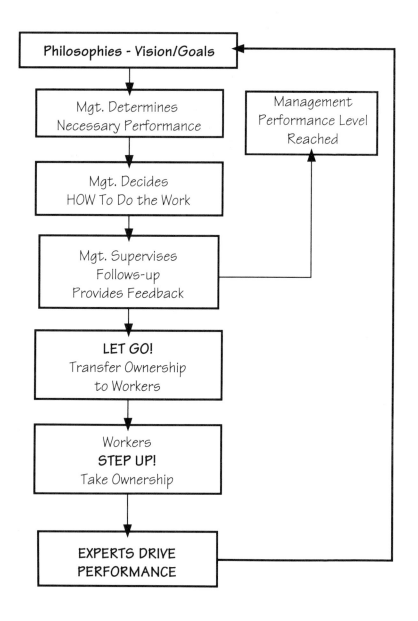

(figure 24)

CONCLUSION

When you get right down to it, people want to contribute. We all want to be valued and respected for our efforts and be part of something successful. The key is to give yourself and co-workers a chance. Let go of the bicycle seat and watch things take off. Step up, become an **Expert** in whatever you do, and encourage others to do the same. Then stand back, great things are headed your way. The sky is the limit.

To all future "Bob the Muffin Men" out there, good luck. Remember, Ownership is a continuous journey. What an adventure!

TAKE POSSESSION,

TAKE CHARGE,

TAKE OWNERSHIP.

YOU ARE THE OWNER!

What You Need to do NOW

Everyone who works for a living:

1. Recognize the situation. Don't let your competitor "pillage your village."
2. Recognize the need for Ownership.
3. Educate yourself. Learn your job. Take an avid interest in it.
4. Become an **Expert** and perform like one. Be the best on the planet at what you do.
5. Build CONFIDENCE, FAITH and TRUST in yourself, your company, your Coach and your co-workers.
6. TAKE Ownership – step up.
7. Spread the word – encourage others, become a catalyst for positive change.

If you're a Coach of any kind, at any level:

1. Recognize the need for Ownership.
2. Commit to the Challenge.
3. Structure your company for Ownership.

   Philosophy and Values

   Vision – Paint the picture

   Jobs – Re-establish how the work is done
4. Educate everyone on the Principles of Ownership.
5. Model Ownership – walk the walk.
6. LET GO.
7. Coach, Coach, Coach.
8. Adjust, Adjust, Adjust.
9. Have FAITH.

THANK YOU FOR READING

THE UNCHAINED WORKER!

JEFFREY PETKEVICIUS

REFERENCES

[1] 1992 Statistical Abstract.

[2] 1992 Business Failure Report, Dunn & Bradstreet.

[3] McConnell, James V. *Understanding Human Behavior*, 3rd ed. New York, NY: Holt, Rinehart and Winston, 1980.

[4] Tice, Lou. *Investment in Excellence for the 90's: Personal Resource Manual*. Seattle, WA: The Pacific Institute, Inc., 1992.

[5] Tice.

ABOUT THE AUTHOR

Jeffrey Petkevicius has led thousands of employees into the Ownership work environment. His experience spans industries from electronics to groceries. Jeff is considered a valuable associate by top executives and rank-and-file employees throughout the U.S. He lives in Spokane, Washington, with his wife and two daughters.